MW00637611

ADVANCE PRAISE

"Deni Naffziger's *Strange Bodies* connects us to a shared humanity and a profound understanding through explorations of time, catastrophe, and emotional interiors. A sophisticated and astute observer, Naffziger retains an exquisite vulnerability akin to Elizabeth Bishop's: 'I believe my consciousness once split / along the seam inside me. / One side a still center, / a steady stone that says I am no different / than a tree, a herd of deer. / The other one reaches for extra salt, / another glass of wine.'"

—Kathleen S. Burgess, author of *The Wonder Cupboard*

"*Strange Bodies* by Deni Naffziger draws on a respect for our identity as flawed humans. In these poems, vision is everything. And we're fortunate to be invited into this examination of whatever we mean by words like *mercy* and *tenderness*. By book's end, I was one of those encouraged to count yellow buses and throw my wrapper out a window. I was giddy with recognition of a shared humanity."

—Roy Bentley, author of *Beautiful Plenty* and *Walking with Eve in the Loved City*, a finalist for the 2018 Miller Williams Poetry Prize

"Deni Naffziger's poems are alive with exploratory courage as she considers the distances between minds and the mystery of the hearts of others. She knows...we live in minds and bodies that are strange to ourselves...[that] [e]ach of us tries to imagine other lives without losing grip on our own identity. This balancing is profoundly recognized in lines about a troubled sister: 'she wished more than once for me to be / inside her head. / But consciousness only goes so far./ Empathy, that flimsy wall, / is all that saved me.'"

—Mark Halliday, author of *Losers Dream On*

"In these intricately wrought poems, Deni Naffziger explores what it means to be an embodied consciousness. From the pen of another writer, this might be abstract, heady stuff, but Naffziger's is a poet's consciousness: 'One side a still center, / a steady stone that says I am no different / than a tree'; the other intensely aware of her singular and connected humanity. *Strange Bodies* indeed, with our blood, tears, and delicate bones; our 'hands, / angular as hex keys'; the 'one hundred trillion cells / and twenty thousand breaths' that 'circulate inside [us] every day' until, of course, they do not. Mortality is at the center of this collection, both birth and death, but the gift of Naffziger's poems is that they offer us that vast and finite space between, 'whether measured in coffee spoons, / or ocean tides and howling moons.'"

—Pauletta Hansel, author of *Heartbreak Tree*, winner of The Poetry Society of Virginia's 2023 Poetry Book Award for North American Writers & Publishers

"*Strange Bodies* gives poetic voice to the act of seeking, exploring what the mind and the self can intuit. Our 'strange bodies,' paradoxically, may be (in part) unknown even to ourselves, but they also may be the only way we are able to access awareness. In much the same way that the science of physics broadens out from finite laws to theoretical questions engaging with infinite potential, this rich collection of poetry asks questions that seem at times essential, at times mysterious, and at times Socratic and philosophical invitations to the reader—always an acknowledgement that the questions are important."

—Bonnie Proudfoot, author of *Goshen Road*, Writers Conference of Northern Appalachia (WCoNA) Book of the Year and long-listed for the 2021 PEN/Hemingway Award

"Some poetry skims across the surface of language as if meaning were an afterthought, but that is not the case with the poems in *Strange Bodies*. These are poems that carry weight, that explore the depth and limits of our understanding and perception in a way that only the most devout reverence for language makes possible."

—James Riley, author of *Broken Frequencies*, recipient of the 2020 Thomas and Lillie D. Chaffin Award for Excellence in Appalachian Literature

Strange

Bodies

ALSO BY DENI NAFFZIGER

Desire to Stay
Still Life
Revenants: A Story of Many Lives (co-authored and funded by the Ohio Arts Council)
A Story of Flying (produced for the Passion Works exhibition, "A Story of Flying")

Strange

DENI NAFFZIGER

Bodies

Shadelandhouse
MODERN PRESS

Lexington, Kentucky

A Shadelandhouse Modern Press book
Strange Bodies
Poems
Copyright © 2023, Text by Deni Naffziger

Published in the United States of America by:

    Shadelandhouse Modern Press, LLC
    Lexington, Kentucky
    smpbooks.com
    Printed in the United States of America
    First edition 2023
Shadelandhouse, Shadelandhouse Modern Press, and the logo are trademarks
of Shadelandhouse Modern Press, LLC.

ISBN: 978-1-945049-36-1 (paperback), 978-1-945049-37-8 (ebook)
Library of Congress Control Number: 2023938281
Cover art: Mark Hackworth
Author photo: Mark Hackworth
"Still Life" photographs: Mark Hackworth
Cover and book design: Iota Books

For Hil and Ella

TABLE OF CONTENTS

Foreword   13

About "Still Life"   17

How Fortunate for a Leaf   21

Strange Bodies   27

Swimming Lessons   29

Druthers   31

Édouard Manet's *Olympia*, A Biography   32

November   33

Little Birds   35

What You Carry   37

In the Direction of Words   39

Last Lesson   41

Abscission   42

Consciousness as a Kind of Relativity   43

The Gift That Came Here   45

Myopia   48

Corkscrew Willow   50

Beneath the Falling Snow   51

Poem to My Younger Self   52

Alias   53

At the River   55

Hands: A Love Story   56

Assignment 61

Chronesthesia: A Time Travel Poem 62

Is It Safe 64

In Delirium: a pantoum 66

Lullaby 68

Apology 69

Metaphor: Letting Go of Guilt 70

A Tale of Two Women 71

Parallax 72

Meditation 74

Confession 75

Forgiveness 76

Aria 77

Eidetic Memory 78

Refugees 79

Absolution 80

Visiting the Warsaw Ghetto 82

Years Later Eucharis Magdalene Speaks to the Blessed Virgin 83

At the Gallery—House on Crescent 84

Yak on the Mountain 85

From the Editor 86

Still Life 91

Acknowledgments 131

About the Author 135

FOREWORD

Entering the consciousness of the poems in Deni Naffziger's *Strange Bodies* is a bit like taking a leap into the spirit of theoretical physics. Imagine each poem as a vibration on the time continuum of the speaker's life.

> ...and on a particular date you will stop thinking of her
> as your mother and instead think of her
> like any other human being or something other
> than human because eventually
> she won't share any of the same qualities you have.
> She will simply be energy at that point.
> And you will ask yourself:
> How does that kind of consciousness work?
>   ("Assignment")

Other notable themes and threads in this collection include human ignorance, the critical role of time in our journey toward awareness and forgiveness, and finally the purpose of aesthetics in our quest to find meaning in what often feels like a random universe. But at the heart of this book is the connection between consciousness and the finite nature of our bodies.

The poems work to answer the question: How does consciousness exist in a mortal body, a body that operates "in total darkness," sometimes "afraid of what [she] do[es] not know" ("Strange Bodies"), especially since "knowing is not real knowing"? ("How Fortunate for a Leaf") From the very start, the speaker understands "How, like the leaf, I often land/without intention/but not without consequence." ("How Fortunate for a Leaf")

To illustrate the mind/body dichotomy, Naffziger often turns to science:

> Even when you sleep...
> one hundred trillion connections

—more than there are stars in the Milky Way—
scramble at two hundred miles per hour...
to deliver this message in the dark:

wake up.

("Strange Bodies")

Of course, "waking up" is what the human journey is all about. The road to awareness may lead to enlightenment, but on the way we may find ourselves more lost than ever, as evidenced by "the dunderhead" whose "witless body betrays itself" before attempting to reconnect with the spirit "on a yearslong journey/to find each other again." ("Strange Bodies") Being mortal while at the same time being part of a larger consciousness is the struggle at the heart of these poems. They celebrate this paradox by asking the reader to look "directly at the lens" ("Edouard Manet's *Olympia*, a Biography") and acknowledge "the line between/sanctuary and danger/at once impalpable." ("November")

Human burdens, such as grief, fear, the need to belong, and others, must be acknowledged and let go. And, like each burden, each poem moves the speaker forward. Her lessons—her daughter's lessons, her son's, her father's—are the readers' lessons. Though each poem stands alone, when read as a collection they resonate like a mantra that invites the reader to transcend individual and even societal issues and to consider them within the broader scope of human experience.

In the poem "Swimming Lessons," time is a lake where a young girl loses her footing on its mossy bottom. She is lucky enough to learn to float—that is, she is alive in the present and, simultaneously, at the moments of her birth and of her mother's death. The lake, one might say, represents the unified field of past, present, and future, where everything happens concurrently:

Then I went under.

How light I felt and unencumbered
as I sank and swam and sailed

beneath her silhouette and listened
to the muffled sound of her heart

as I must have heard it long ago
when I was weightless, unaware.

Why does any of this matter? The poems address how small and yet how connected we are to one another, to the planet, and beyond. They illustrate not only the limits of consciousness as it clings to a body but also how the search for *knowing* creates a capacity for forgiveness and ultimately an acceptance of abundance. Consequently, *Strange Bodies* is uplifting in its insights and resonates with hope.

Poems positioned later in the manuscript reveal how self-knowledge (and knowledge of the world around us) is delivered from one generation to the next. The burden of knowledge—even that of cell memory—grows heavier as our mortal bodies age. Passing it along to our children provides relief, and what was once a burden becomes a gift.

In "Chronesthesia: A Time Travel Poem," the past, present, and future are not depicted in a linear fashion, and the universe becomes the ultimate gift when the indifference of a natural world provides hope:

Science says the energy that powers all life
survives through transformation.

...somewhere
he was flying out of bed in the morning,
playing alone in the catalpa grove, dancing
with an Irish girl on the campus green.

...With each journey another clue:
wild, orange lilies, *boots cracking like gunfire...*

But enough about backward travel and the paradox
it presents when our future appears as our past.
We all know our children will leave us...
as if they can solve the mystery of their lives...
smiling, from the present tense.

In the poem "From the Editor," the artist's role in a conscious world is made clear:

...I thought, too, about how we waste our very best years
trying to create meaning, how we hope
to balance the poet's desire with the publisher's standard...
...we are
the narcissus in the yard,
pushing through the frozen earth.
When we finally do break through,
how little time we have!...
...What is our calling, after all,
if not to be astonished?

In a final wake-up call to notice the astonishing world around us, Naffziger provides a convergence of the beauty of the natural world, the hope provided by forgiveness, and the celebration of an open and vibrant consciousness. Being home in a world not always comprehensible, she reflects on her capacity to forgive and be forgiven—and that opens the door for the rest of us.

—Jane Ann Fuller, author of *Half-Life*, 2021 National Indie Excellence Awards finalist

ABOUT "STILL LIFE"

The last section of the book, "Still Life," is a composite of eight poems, several of which appear as individual pieces or as parts of longer poems in the collection, and these have been edited to form a single reflection. *Still Life*, a biography of existence in word and image, was completed during the 2020 pandemic lockdown and mirrors conversations between the poet, Deni Naffziger, and her husband, photographer Mark Hackworth, about the role of beauty and aesthetics in the day to day, as a way to create meaning in the absence of time. The work was originally conceived as a nineteen-piece series of framed prints, each exhibited to appear as open pages of a book. The exhibition made its debut at University of Pikeville (Pikeville, Kentucky), with exhibitions following at The Secret Studio (Columbus, Ohio), The Dairy Barn Arts Center (Athens, Ohio), and Praxis Gallery (Minneapolis, Minnesota). Before its second showing, the series was made into a fine art book that now serves as an accompaniment at exhibitions. In the introduction to *Still Life*, James Riley, author of *Broken Frequencies*, writes:

> [*Still Life* illustrates] the present and the past caught in a single moment of experience where both, like language or a photographic image, achieve meaning in an otherwise meaningless sequence of events. In such an environment, a crumpled sheet of paper becomes a flower, a speckled egg a dead bird... [T]he arc of our understanding has the ability to connect these disparate images from where we begin, in the midst of misunderstanding, to, hopefully, where we end, conscious and aware and in search of some form of forgiveness, not from the world around us but from ourselves. This is the journey of *Still Life*, a simple image becoming landscape becoming our access to the sublime.

Strange Bodies

HOW FORTUNATE FOR A LEAF

to drop like wisdom
from the arm of its mother
to land without foresight or fear
having lived only
              ever
                  in the present
How I am learning
        that knowing is not real
                  knowing
nor ignorance either
How choosing is a choice I'd rather not make
sometimes
How not choosing
is a choice I don't know I'm making
How like the leaf I often land
without intention
but not without consequence

"The body knows."

Final entry in the journals of Mary Naffziger

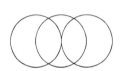

STRANGE BODIES

1.

The fact of the matter is
your body operates in total darkness.
What is permitted by nature, or evolutionary biology,
or perhaps by God, are two slight openings
with which to see everything.
Meanwhile one hundred trillion cells
and twenty thousand breaths
circulate inside you every day.
Even when you sleep,
even when you dream you are climbing
an ancient tree in your neighbor's yard
to reach for the magnolia blossom,
and your long monkey feet wrap around the trunk,
even as you fall with a flower in your hand
and your husband calls from the kitchen
and the smell of toast and coffee is what you least expect
in the cloud forest you fall from,
eighty-six billion nerve cells,
and one hundred trillion connections
—more than there are stars in the Milky Way—
scramble at two hundred miles per hour
over a distance of sixty-thousand miles,
twice the circumference of planet earth inside you,
to deliver this message in the dark:

wake up.

2.

Sometimes you are afraid of what you do not know.
Sometimes you stand on the back patio at night,
look through trees and hear a colorless hum that hides
between whip-poor-will and memory,
soon lost in the babble of after-dark arias:
the grand nocturnal opera,
its principal players hiding all around you.
And you, in full view, the dunderhead.
This must be how the spirit feels,
long after its arrival
when the witless body betrays itself
and the two become strangers on a yearslong journey
to find each other again.

SWIMMING LESSONS

I never did learn to swim at the Y
with other skinny first-grade girls

in bright red regulation suits,
yanked high at the shoulders –

straps wrapped tight with rubber bands.
We stood like prisoners at the locker room mirror,

that little *V* between the legs, obscene
(if a 6-year old can know what obscenity is).

And the concave space between the suit and groin –
a humiliation. For just a minute

I cozied up to another girl
for protection more than friendship, and together

we made our way through humid, chlorinated air
to the pool where we were tested.

Like the others, I leaned forward in the water,
head down, hands pressed together like the bow of a ship.

One foot discreetly hopped along the bottom.
The other, the stern, pretended to float.

It wasn't until one day at Farmer Jim's,
a manmade lake where kids splashed unattended

while mothers unpacked sandwiches
and babysitters flirted with the guards,

that my feet first slipped on the mossy floor
and I swam by mistake.

Years later, after my mother died,
I dreamed we swam together in a pond.

Children's voices lifted like fog
and she fell back across my arms.

Her face reflected April skies, blue eyes
and white hair drifting toward another season.

Then I went under.

How light I felt and unencumbered
as I sank and swam and sailed

beneath her silhouette and listened
to the muffled sound of her heart

as I must have heard it long ago
when I was weightless, unaware.

DRUTHERS

I prefer mad love to mad anything else,
tea above coffee, silent mornings overall.
I prefer winter to spring,
its short-lived sun blasting the window
without apology or mitigation of leaves.
I prefer October over any other month:
grass crackle and root vegetables,
the way each and every starling in a murmuration
is connected – more physics than biology.
I prefer physics to biology, and quarks to protons,
illusive, ethereal clouds of energy
that cannot be measured
like waves of love or grief.
Which is not to say they don't exist.
I prefer remembering my mother
under Long Nights Moon,
her diaphanous skin,
the arc of a life in her spine.

EDOUARD MANET'S *OLYMPIA*, A BIOGRAPHY

Most women would never
climb over a row of seats at the opera house,
but my mother did and she was old
or what you might *call* old, with delicate bones
and a stylish, starch-white bob.
My sister and I were surprised (if not embarrassed)
but others were dazzled.
My father, he was incredulous
though I'm not sure why;
Mother rarely did what was expected.
After all she stayed with him,
and no one saw that coming.
All those nights in Warren, Ohio,
when he sat out back in his underwear,
grilling steaks and the very tenets of Catholicism
(he, himself, a convert who faked it badly for years),
the neighbors couldn't imagine in their wildest dreams
the two of them driving west,
drinking beer outside the Winnebago,
naming constellations, or stumbling
up my grandparents' stairs in the dark,
my mother laughing; then silence.
Then audible fucking.
As a girl she played on the wing of Amelia Earhart's plane,
a detail she shared years later,
like any other, like her hair was once red,
like she wore a meal-sack dress
the day her father took a picture,
and she looked directly at the lens.

NOVEMBER

It is November
and the child's socks are falling down.

On Cranbrook Circle,
houses appear quiet outside.

Inside,
the girl's mother plays Moonlight Sonata.

Her metronome spine
a kind of solace

against the chaos of murder
in Dallas.

Television images of people crying—
like her mother crying,

following notes on a page,
knowing exactly

what sound comes next
and when—

slip into the house, subtle as memory:
a continuum of black and white.

The line between
sanctuary and danger

at once impalpable.
Is life this uncertain?

LITTLE BIRDS

1.

The story begins with my mother at the ironing board
just after the death of her preterm infant, and a boy
from my 3rd grade class who has come to play.
Wallpaper covers the hallway walls, misty-green
Eiffel towers floating in amnion sacs, and just beyond
the rounded arch that separates us from her,
she stands crying in the living room.
Her thin lips trill, and tears fall onto my father's shirt
that hangs, disengaged, until she starches it.
Then bit by bit it stiffens –
the collar, the cuffs.
The boy and I move past her grief
to the yard where wild raspberries grow.
We hold them like little birds in our hands,
delight in the bitter and the sweet.
By the time we finish, what remains of the berries
are clots between our fingers.

2.

My daughter calls to tell me she is miscarrying
and baking a cake as we speak. I picture her
measuring flour, sugar, and cream.
Layers of sorrow and loss, anguish and longing
blend seamlessly in the yellow bowl.
My mother never baked when menstruating
for fear the batter would lie flat
in the pan. My daughter is fearless,
holds no regard for superstition.

Even as she bleeds, she pours
the mix into four stainless-steel bowls,
stirs calculated ratios of blue and red into each,
a progression of color: lavender to heather,
iris to violet.

3.

I look for clarity,
for meaning and reassurance,
interpretation (a bit of history, even)
in the dictionary. All the words are there
or most of the ones I might ever use. Still,
a zebrafish will never know what it's like to be a monkey.
A rabbit will never see inside a tangle of trees
or what whirligig beetles see from any one or more
of their many eyes. I don't know either,
but I can try.

4.

And what about those babies in jars
at the Chicago Museum of Science
and Industry all lined up on a shelf,
nine jars, one for each month, to illustrate
the development of an embryo?
Where did they come from,
and who decided to put them in jars,
to display them at a museum for young
visitors to study? Even as a child,
I wondered *where were their mothers*.

WHAT YOU CARRY

For J.A.

In third grade I ran away from home
with a handful of crackers and a few Nik-L-Nip
wax bottles filled with sugar water all snug
inside a blue bandana that was tied to a stick.
Before I reached the end of the block,
the bandana kept sliding down the stick,
just looked ridiculous, so I untied it,
shoved everything into my pockets
and tossed the limb into a yard.

When I finally left home for good,
I was tempted to steal a Cumbrian teacup
from my mother's shelf but realized the joy
was in the ritual of steeping and sipping.
I didn't need to steal anything.
Oh but I could go on about all I wanted
to take from my mother, like the emerald ring
she wore on her right hand. Instead
I ended up with her hands
that moved like birds in the air
when she told stories at the table.

Your mother is dying now.
She no longer needs stories
or tables, or food for that matter.
She has tossed it all in the yard
on her way to someplace else.
What will remain is all that she left –
water on the bedside table.

Hulls littering the ground.
Those birds whose survival
will always be more beautiful to us
than our own.

IN THE DIRECTION OF WORDS

The nursing home chef prepared
sliced turkey, canned green beans,
boxed mashed potatoes with gravy –
all iridescent under hospital light.
My father hadn't spoken for weeks,
but the day before he died
he was lively.

I fed him little spoonsful
as he nattered on about dead relatives
who'd come to visit that afternoon.
He and his father fixed a reel-to-reel,
while his son-in-law explained
why Federico Fellini mattered.
And Professor Dave,
my mother's father, sat silent
on a wooden chair beside the window –
never answered a single question
my father asked.

Two years earlier,
I'd driven him home from hospital,
following open-chest surgery.
Visors and sunglasses protected
our eyes from snow and more snow
and January light reflecting off drifts
when he told me a secret.

On their honeymoon, my mother cried
after making love for the first time.

She wore flannel pajamas.
Though he made no mention of blood,
I could tell he felt bad about that night.
She had been so unprepared.

Which brings me to my own confession:
after I pulled the spoon through his lips
for what (I didn't realize) would be the very last time,
I looked out the little metal-framed window,
saw a handful of cars under snow.
I imagined my husband at home
loading wood into the stove, gently
sliding the old dog on the tile floor
away from anywhere ash might land.
I will admit I wanted to leave.
The room smelled like dirty adult diapers.
Muted on the television, a male dancer
pranced across the black and white screen.
My father was staring at the ceiling again,
his mouth open, his tongue moving
in the direction of words when I stood
to put on my coat and he asked:
Do I have to go?

LAST LESSON

Do you remember
when he tipped you back,
held your head
in the cup of his hand –
your arms wide,
eyes fixed
on seabirds
and swallows?
Now he has let go
and you are prepared
as he intended
for the riptide that pulls you
to the ocean floor
like a star fish caught
between gravity
and weightlessness. The body
knows its pharyngeal gills
trade water for remembrance.
You will breathe like this
for weeks or months
or longer
and when you return
waves of grief will find you
making your mother's bed.
Drop everything since nothing
can fight the force of water.
Ask rocks and rivers
how many tears
it took to shape
the shore.

ABSCISSION

When I think of secrets
I think of my grandmother
and the hidden staircase I followed
from her bedroom closet to the mudroom,
to the open, unused well outside,
its black mouth wide and silent,
an old corkscrew willow in the yard,
so many leaf scars, and the tornado that lifted
the entire suffering thing straight out of the ground.
I think of the attic filled with her son's belongings,
every letter he ever wrote to her, the hair of dead children
in boxes between rafters, and tiny turn-of-the-century shoes.
If all the sins and secrets of the world were fallen leaves,
they would soften the road from her farm in central Illinois
to the foothills of eastern Colorado. Her son's murdered body
riding undisturbed in the boot of a Ford Fairlane.
At dawn, the sun burns red, a sailor's warning,
as a deputy sheriff makes his rounds to the tune
of *Don't Be Cruel*. Flies buzz
above the trunk of a car in a motel parking lot
at 5 AM—Nothing can prepare you for some things.
In fourth grade, I learned about abscission,
a river birch in summer, each leaf connected to the tree
like a son to his mother. When the leaf drops,
what remains is a scar that heals over,
can barely be seen.

CONSCIOUSNESS AS A KIND OF RELATIVITY

When I was 5-years old, I dreamed I was 6.
I woke to throw back the quilt on my mother's bed
(since that is where I often slept)
and ran downstairs, out the backdoor,
onto my big, red bike.
I pedaled up Crescent Drive –
prodigious elms overhead, and sunlight
made its way beneath the canopy.
I was 6-years old and fully alive,
breathing in, as if for the first time,
the sweet air of ginger grass.
I awoke from that dream in my mother's bed.
Great breaths of quiet wafted between
my brother's angry cries and the clank
of silverware downstairs.
Was I five or was I six?
Was I sleeping still? Was my life real?
How could I know?

My sister's dolls were put away like sick children.
Naked babies sat on shelves in her room
with blue ink numbers scribbled on their vinyl heads
– smudged from kissing.
Surgeries she called them.
When we were old and she was sick with voices
she wished more than once for me to be
inside her head.
But consciousness only goes so far.
Empathy, that flimsy wall,

is all that saved me.
I was, thankfully, alone in my own.

I believe my consciousness once split
along the seam inside me.
One side a still center,
a steady stone that says I am no different
than a tree, a herd of deer.
The other one reaches for extra salt,
another glass of wine.

THE GIFT THAT CAME HERE

Hawaiian translation for "ukulele"

1. Ohana - *family*

Unlike a common guitar,
the ukulele is a small instrument,
the curved body of which seeks comfort
against my thigh, my belly and breast;
this tiny body, attenuated neck, finds no repose.
I hold it like a mother holds her own peculiar child,
like our mother held you in the winter of 1960.
And so it is that struggle I remember
the day she brought you home:
the redolent scent of Clementine,
a reminder that fresh fruit grows elsewhere but not here
in December, and the light outside, nearly blinding.
Finally, your strangeness bound
in a white cotton blanket across the room,
the memory of Christmas
as real as a wooden horse on springs
when I envied you.

2. Ha'ina - *the song is almost over*

16 hours of uninterrupted sleep
legs that barely carry you
from bed to sofa to smoke
another cigarette
your laundry in the corner
pockets matted with cash

cigarette butts old notes forgotten
reminders to look up seize the day
smile little monkey
no caffeine but just once
or one more
and who would know?
Except that knowing is too much to bear
and so confession.

3. Hana Hou – *Encore*

two cups of coffee, another cigarette,
your mom on the phone your dad
won't dress himself won't even try
his left eye blind
his legs don't work your own legs
weaker by the minute
what happens
if too much is stuck inside your head
and you can't get it out?
will it kill me?
another cigarette
another nap to a cartoon soundtrack
dreams of diving into the hotel pool
weightless
eyes closed and water
seeps into your lungs like a mole
who knows a secret you don't know
a secret that could save you
if you could learn to swim

4. A hui hou - *until we meet again*

Sister would I trade places with you if I could? Would I
live different in the hope that you might understand me
despite my otherness?
Would spastic muscles in my legs, taut as ukulele strings,
let loose a song that might lead you to know me?
You are my first memory, and to this day we are dissonant notes
floating on the wave of our mother's breath.
Her oldest child, I nurture you like a lesson
I have not yet come to learn, like an instrument
I practice again and again, that I sing along with
when no one is listening.

MYOPIA

Boynton Road blossoms on the hillside with sweet william.
Like children, once alive, it billows beneath an insistent

cloud of memory where a boy once appeared at our farm
for water. The chemicals would have killed us

had we stayed. Crop dusters sprayed in July, and we,
like angels or insects, followed our cousins into a toxic dust.

We plucked, strung, and swallowed Mary Leigh's beans;
bathed, three at a time, in the clawfoot tub and crawled into bed.

Over the downstairs murmur of our parents drinking highballs,
we mocked the boy, Arthur, and his raffish laugh.

I was afraid of him or attracted,
being too young to know the difference.

I thought about his summer-colored skin,
the entire length of him spread out like a map to parts unknown.

If we existed in a parallel universe, I might have stayed where I came from
but crickets sang a song of longing that carried me into unfamiliar sleep.

Arthur recounted the day and each one of us pretending
to see him as he wanted to see himself. Only now do I see

I have always been running
through rows of corn with tassels overhead;

bits of blue sky, an illusion, as thunderheads form out of vapor
and blow across the field without warning.

CORKSCREW WILLOW

Dust blows across the field under a dispassionate sun.
Men on machines in the field work like ants.
Cancer is everywhere.
A punching bag hangs from an old oak
beside the coop. A rooster in the yard
scares all the new chickens. Listen:
a cat is locked in the corncrib,
its insistent bellow barely audible
against the wind, the dust, the men on machines.
Miles and miles of toxic beans
and in the great distance, clumps of trees
hold on like family. I read old letters
to my cousin in the living room
on a couch covered with satin cloth.
Her horses stare at us through a window
and in the great distance,
men on machines and dust that blows
and blows across cancerous fields.
She is the soul of this place. The one
who sacrificed a seemingly perfect
breast — two years later a kidney.
She planted maples from seed,
snapped six willow sprigs
from our (long-dead) grandfather's tree,
trusting that one might prosper.

BENEATH THE FALLING SNOW

If this day were a photograph,
no one would ask how we came to be here,
why she bellowed from beyond the frozen pond,
how I strained to see the unseeable deep within the woods
but stopped short of entering alone.

I returned with the slick, black dog that ran ahead.
An injured doe had made her way across the dam.
She lay in shock beneath the falling snow.
One brown eye blinked to protect the smallest bit of her,
but the blood, which would not be veiled, drained from her body
and a gray mist drifted toward the dog.

What point is fear — the distant pain
that bleeds its way toward lilacs
that will never bloom in her lifetime?
Instinct and imagination are different animals.
I have one and not the other. I brought a dog to protect me
from what I do not know, and I cannot smell the future.

In a few short months, male cardinals will call out "birdie, birdie, birdie."
Goddamn ants will rise up from the soil, and geese will line the shore.
It may snow in April, but Forsythia never panics.

POEM TO MY YOUNGER SELF

By the time you arrive you will know
what I know or more than I know
if you listen to song sparrows
singing in the orchard and indigo buntings
inviting you beneath a canopy of leaves
where black-billed cuckoos lurk
in the undergrowth.
When days grow short, heed the trill
of the dark-eyed junco and the nasal call
of the sandhill crane who insist
that you pull a coat from the closet,
your socks from the drawer.

Every season surprised me.
I only heard the voice that said *you will never*
be stunning like a scarlet tanager,
or regal like a peacock. You will never
sing like a wood thrush
or think like a wild hooded crow.
You're not as clever as a kea,
and the red-capped manakin
couldn't teach you to dance
if its life depended on it.
As strange as it sounds,
that voice is a bird inside your head,
pecking at the shell to get beyond you.
Listen.

ALIAS

What would you make of a girl
who tossed a parakeet into the ceiling,

who cut open carpet beetles with a common steak knife,
observed their insides were like wet Kleenex

and asked: *where is the heart?*
She knew her eyes

were the only place in her body where light refracted.
The rest of her remained in darkness.

I loved that curious girl and set out to find her
on the internet. I found myself

scrolling through a lifetime in digital data
calling out from an analogue age,

pictures I thought I'd discarded when I left that century behind.
Yet here was proof: my baptism

at St. Mary's church, my sisters and I
in cotton pajamas, cradling Tiny Tears dolls

in front of the silver tree at Christmas.
There was the son I held

though not nearly enough and the dog I walked
beside the pond who stopped to admire

starlings in the tops of trees. The truth is
I have been a stranger to myself.

I have regret and regret is a dolorous ride
in a 1975 Plymouth Fury

from which I never once observed a single tree
lost in the blur of motion.

AT THE RIVER

I have taught my son the importance of smell,
of holding a spoor in the back of his throat
while ordinary air
filters its way to his lungs
like he has no eyes
the way his breath captures light,
folds it away,
studies the loam of a speckled stone,
a broken shell in the dark.
Fish odor rises like prayer.
He will remember it was autumn,
the dishes having just been done,
the scent of them on and around me
as we play like stone statues moving freely
on the bank. Trees thin
and the road we traveled to get here
dims. This night at the river
he throws rocks in like words
that narrate a brackish whiff
of tidal marsh we inhale
and will hold onto.

HANDS: A LOVE STORY

Do you remember the night our cat nearly drowned?
You thrust your hands beneath the ice.

They came out wild and waxen as the eyes of a dove.
Shimmered like promise.

I hold your hands and the rhythm of my heart
becomes the wind off Angel Ridge.

When you fill the mallards' pail, it rattles
hunger until they waddle to the feed,

pecking, pecking a frantic pulse.
I'd plan my own death with an escape hatch if I could

to touch either of those hands,
angular as hex keys, driving bolts and screws.

You invent the word *shelter*
when you swing hammer to nail, steadier

than white half-runners scaling summer.
Our pond is elegant in the fashion of your hands:

coffers with hidden drawers that open without warning.
Mysterious things. Like birds.

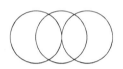

"The whole cosmos was infinitely less than the whole of being...
the whole infinity of being underlay every moment of the cosmos."
Olaf Stapledon, *Star Maker*

ASSIGNMENT

Draw a timeline.   Begin
with your birth and your mother
who wove stories to bind you to her.
End with your death and ignore imagination.
You cannot forecast cause:
brain cancer or heart attack in the produce aisle.
Nor can you predict setbacks
like crying at your first job interview
or drinking too much afterwards.
A timeline allows you to visualize
significant achievements:
graduation, employment, your wedding day,
and so on and so forth until many years later
when you learn about Andromeda
and other galaxies and their relationship to you.
Like your relationship to your mother
who will surely have died by then,
and on a particular date you will stop thinking of her
as your mother and instead think of her
like any other human being or something other
than human because eventually
she won't share any of the same qualities you have.
She will simply be energy at that point.
And you will ask yourself:
How does that kind of consciousness work?

CHRONESTHESIA: A TIME TRAVEL POEM

I left my home 10,000 years ago and I pine for those I love...alive and dead.
—Jacqueline Boyle, *Time Travel Journals*

[T]he distinction between the past, present, and future is only a stubbornly persistent illusion.
—Albert Einstein

Do you remember how dinosaurs lumbered
through forests and flood plains,
foraging for food, speaking in hoots,
howls, and crackling sounds 370 days a year?
Not that they were counting.

And the moon, like a hovering mother,
distanced herself as days, weeks, months,
years, decades, centuries, millennia passed.
18-hour days plodded their way to 24.
Years fell short.   Time
is just another sibling, you know,
born in a bang along with the rest of us
some 13 billion years ago.
Don't tell me we weren't witness.
Science says the energy that powers all life
survives through transformation.

As a young man my father was all salt and swagger.
Before he died, he was small as we talked about physics
and what we barely understood but held onto
in the hopes that our limited understanding of string theory,
cyclical time, and hallucinations meant that somewhere

he was flying out of bed in the morning,
playing alone in the catalpa grove, dancing
with an Irish girl on the campus green.
We travel this way for many reasons.
My friend has ventured hundreds of times
to the woods her husband traipses from his truck
to the tree where he shoots himself. Again
and again. With each journey another clue:
wild, orange lilies, *boots cracking like gunfire*.
I often return to the bicycle I ride at full speed,
bare-chested, still a girl. Boys race to overcome me,
to look back at my little nipples, while girls
on the sideline titter like Carolina wrens.

But enough about backward travel and the paradox
it presents when our future appears as our past.
We all know our children will leave us,
find us less interesting, move across town
and beyond, to go traveling through time
as if they can solve the mystery of their lives
or take strength in that distant self who waves,
smiling, from the present tense.

IS IT SAFE

to put a pond in a poem?
How about a heron at the shoreline,
its leg lifted like a mime
over unsuspecting carp?

Is it safe to slip a snail in a pond
in a poem spilling over with algae?
What about a promise? Will it float
like hope? Will it glimmer and flash,
arouse curiosity or worse?

I once slung a secret in a pond in a poem.
It grew a tail, a carapace and bony plates,
a beak with a rough cutting edge.
It took on a life of its own,
ripped the legs right off a cricket frog,
tore the head off a lotus,
spread rumors I never intended.

I wonder what a memory would do?
If I tossed it like a stone,
would it skip, sink, or swim?
Would it drown or dwarf or morph
into something more or less
like love,
like loss,
like regret?

What about sun on the surface, a kingfisher
diving for truth? The red-winged blackbird
so far away he's nearly
left the page?

IN DELIRIUM: A PANTOUM

Fourteen thousand years ago
a star called Vela died.
I try to organize my days.
I can no longer organize my days.

A star called Vela died.
It rivered through the atmosphere and I
try to organize my days
by trees and lakes and ocean coral.

Whatever rivers through the atmosphere,
however random, is measured now
in trees and lakes and ocean coral.
What should I study for evidence?

Time is measured by fitful reminders
of what I lost, evidence
of a life in hindsight:
round fingertips, nails bitten to the nub.

Reminded of what I have lost,
I imagine myself without a body.
Round fingertips, nails bitten to the nub no more!
My phantom breath a temporary vestige.

Without a body, my limbs
are shattered stars blasting cosmic radiation
through every breath I ever took.
Time is a fourth dimension, a necessary coordinate.

Shattered stars blast cosmic radiation,
turned by time, buried beneath sediment.
Time is a fourth dimension
that tells me where I am.

Buried by time, turned beneath sediment,
is proof of a star called Vela.
I miss the only coordinate that matters.
I can no longer organize my days.

LULLABY

When you slept, the entire house rested on your breath,
barely audible, like a secret about all you knew before.

I had forgotten the suffering until you woke to remind me
that outside the cradle of our house, beyond the gladiolus and larkspur,

many were not so safely tucked between the sheets.
There were little bones and tears,

broken glass and uninvited laughter; while overhead Andromeda,
Cassiopeia, and Cepheus remained indifferent.

Sometimes in the crib you startled as if you were falling from an unnamed galaxy,
so fast and afraid your spirit left its body incognizant.

Years later I stood at my mother's bed, her mouth slack but not angry at me
for arriving late—her death a private milestone.

O daughter, how I remembered you then,
so very long ago: asleep beneath my vigilant eye,

still tethered to that same ethereal landscape
from which you were delivered.

APOLOGY

This much I know:
you died without warning,

except there is always warning.
 What I don't know or can't recall:

everything else, really –
whether the oak had turned, or the hickory,

the mood, like sky for all I remember.

I walk down the lane in winter
and long for a different season.

Finches, doves, meadowlarks commence
their singing while cranes and killdeer

return unnoticed by longspurs and harriers
who, like me, are poised

for a journey we anticipate far too long.
When it arrives, I rather prize the song

of a white-throated sparrow
trilling *Oh Canada* from this Ohio tree.

METAPHOR: LETTING GO OF GUILT

I dreamed I killed a bee—
a brutal assassination.

To begin
I laid the little thing on his back,
sawed off his legs with considerable effort.
    Nothing left but stumps.
Figured he'd bleed out
(though he did not).
He was as angry as a hornet,
so I took him up behind the neck
(like a mama cat carries her young)
to toss him into the pond.
But this was no kitten!
His triangle head, baring enormous teeth,
lurched toward my arm,
as if to bite me. Then over the water
he soared as I watched from shore
with only mild remorse
as he worked hard to stay afloat,
bobbing toward the spillway.

A TALE OF TWO WOMEN

Today I make gazpacho while Joe is dying.
My husband picks tomatoes and cucumbers,

carries them to the kitchen like he always does.
I peel oxhearts. Billie holds her husband's hand,

traces the soft spaces between his tendons,
circles the bone of his wrist

while I slice vegetables into quarters,
then eighths, then turn them

from vertical to horizontal.
She empties the urinal, and I

scoop seeds from the cutting board,
wipe it dry.

An entire jalapeño seems too much,
so I halve it. Another dose

of morphine, a plague of grackles
in the garden.

PARALLAX

You can't write about the spaces between
without acknowledging history,
whether it takes place in a living room
when an older cousin comes to call
or atop a Saturn V at Launch Complex 39A
where a 363-foot rocket will cast 3 men
into the annals of exploration.
In the latter case, an entire nation understands
what it bears witness to, but at home
three young girls line up in front of a piano,
lift their nightshirts, exposing bare feet,
knob knees, and white cotton undies.
Apollo 11 has cleared the tower,
orbits earth in a sea of tranquility.
The girls, too, orbit a sphere which,
by definition, should be as familiar
as their own planet earth, as a glass
of Jim Beam in their father's hand,
and the farmland accent of a cousin
who is as comfortable in suburban Ohio
as in a cattle barn. Fireflies drift slowly
around the ship, 7 or 8 feet apart,
carry the men on starlight wings.
The astronauts name them neither angels
nor aliens—but observe,
then document.
Meanwhile the children float
in their own extraneous present
as the spaces between their legs are measured
like the distance between what we know

and what we don't yet recognize.
Who do terrestrial daughters report to
while their fathers navigate celestial globes?
How do they measure the parallax of experience
years later when they gaze at a hunger moon
and remember?

MEDITATION

Of course we will collide with Andromeda. Of course
everyone and everything will die and be reborn.
Your head ends here, but where does your mind end?
Something is lost in the back of it amid dark matter,
expanding what you can't quite put your finger on,
eluding you, slipping under the fence and running off to the fair
with big ideas about flight, bright light, and distraction.
Once you had a dog who tiptoed behind you
— short, slick-black fur, looked like a shadow running beneath the moon.
The woods brightly lit, patterns morphed on the forest floor
and she followed close. Next morning you found a gift at the door:
the small clay head of a child that now sits on a cabinet.
My point is this: it's easy to drift with your head in the clouds.
Forget about space. Hold on to January,
when memory of first snow and holidays fade,
when dark-eyed junco and the old blind squirrel compete for seed,
when your feet can no longer stand the idea of themselves without socks
and the pups look like prisoners at the window. You see a girl
become a bird and a bird become something
neither of us recognize, an apparition, a far-flung galaxy
advancing like there is no tomorrow.

CONFESSION

"A confession has to be part of your new life."
—Ludwig Wittgenstein

Birds tossed into living room ceilings.
Dogs run over in driveways.
Cats (who knows where your father took them?).
Fish flushed.
Ferrets stuffed and placed on the mantel
or buried outside in Tupperware.
You improvised elaborate rituals,
eulogized an animal's better nature.

Still, it hurt
when you found the rabbit dead
in the backyard pen.
You suspected your neighbor, Dicky Thomas—
only to learn, years later, it was your brother
who broke its spine.
People change
though some would argue
a child who kills a rabbit
will suffer redemption.

Tonight under palm trees and full-flower moon,
far from the steelworks of your childhood home,
your brother admits he once witnessed the spirit
relinquish the body—a body that lived without malice
when he dropped a stone in the hutch,
and a seed that festered inside him took root,
blossomed like a thousand apologies.

FORGIVENESS

He smoked Pall Malls with abandon,
a bottle of Jim Beam cinched between
his thighs, Dean Martin on the radio
singing to the five of us
little kids in the back seat. So what?
So he bought us all fast food, crumpled
the empty bags and tossed them out the window
like what he'd rather forget, then told us
to toss ours too, and we all lined up on our knees,
looked out the wide expanse of rearview window,
watched wads of garbage flit like orchids.
Sometimes we fought like dogs, and he paid us
to count yellow school buses in July to shut us up.
We were young. He was too, in a reckless age,
and eventually those empty bags,
all those cigarette butts that tumbled
from the ashtray along the outside
of his green Fleetwood, Jim Beam turned upside down,
smashed on the pavement and sparkling like fairy dust,
were miles and miles behind us.

ARIA

We are given the tree, roots tangled,
brown and tender like a house wren
choking from the tree hole:
I can't breathe.

It's an anthem rooted at the heart
of an ailing planet, a dirge hell-bent
on coaxing the woodcutter to unlock
the shed out back, to grab the ax.

Our inheritance is a nest infested
with parasites that feed on blinded chicks.
With our mother gone, what should we do
but fill the roost with spiders,

then listen for an effervescent voice,
the rush-and-jumble song that hope employs?

EIDETIC MEMORY

Elephants emerged from the waters of Moeris
to the rhythm of a melody their progeny sing.
Footprints were secrets the oceans kept safe.
But the earth remembers.

Amid egrets, cichlids, coelacanth, and bushpig,
they slumbered beneath mangosteen and sausage trees,
their canopy lit by stars as rivers snaked their way
into the great Zambezi, and the fires of Toba
buried all but the planet's recollection
of moon orchid, dahlia, and rose.

Millions of years later
a sun-bleached mastodon
on yellowed grass
is excavated, its imprint
a complicated narrative of discovery:
song, celebration, apology, and regret.
But not yet forgiveness.

REFUGEES

Why only remember the ones who perished
in hot ash and pumice, their lungs on fire,
faces covered with pillows and cloth,
who refused to leave when blue skies
darkened black as obsidian,
and tall, broad flames blazed from Vesuvius?
Maybe because
plaster cast bodies tell stories we cannot erase
of a sky mottled and dirty with earth,
of men and women calling for each other
in the dark as the sea shallowed
and left sunfish stranded on dry sand.
What of those who have nothing to lose
or everything to lose and leave anyway,
who abandon plates full of olives
and fava beans rattling on tables,
who interrupt the songs of their children,
invent new songs as they run with them
past outdoor markets and bakeries
with sun-gold loaves of sourdough
still in the oven, past bright yellow frescoes
of foliage and fowl?
What of wood pigeons and sparrows,
blue rock thrush, golden orioles and even
that harbinger of trouble, the black-billed magpie,
who leads the way and no one thinks to praise or blame?
Clouds sink behind them and cover the sea.
It is daylight everywhere else.

ABSOLUTION

I

Since the pandemic, I don't see my daughter.
She stays in another house, in a different town.
I imagine her living a life with her husband,
the two of them painting their walls *Du Jour*,
or planting peonies by the fence row—
how we calm ourselves after a loved one departs.
For now, I plan warm-weather visits
when we will sit a safe distance in the yard
or swim in the chlorinated pool where germs and viruses die
and we will hug underwater.

II

My cousin's son was shot dead on hallowed ground,
on land our family owned for generations,
where the family tree was rooted.
I wrote her a letter that said: *For a long time*
you may feel like you are walking under water.
I think about her thinking about him as a child
and as a man. She has all the time in the world
to reminisce about him with his grandfather now,
and grandmother, gathering white-half-runners
in a field where it will always be late July,
and with his great uncle who was murdered in Chicago,
and the other one who refused to sell the family farm to her
so that a stranger would buy it and one day
shoot her boy beneath the corkscrew willow.

III

They have forgiven themselves and each other
because *heaven* is where lessons have already been learned.
It's how we sometimes manage to forgive ourselves
on this planet,
believing one day we will be absolved,
and one day she will hug her son again,
stroke the soft, fine fibers of his auburn hair
and I will hold my daughter
again
and remember how we waited
for the end of waiting.

VISITING THE WARSAW GHETTO

We pictured our ancestors building walls
under strict and violent guard
as the dutiful sky hovered like a mother,
her breezes gently reminding us we are all pushed
from the door with hesitation,
even on a sun-soaked day, the very day
we crept among the ghosts
of our grandfathers who were burned
then covered with dirt and merciful rain.
Six million makes it easy to ignore
one man's suffering. Many are tired
of this: our story, our sadness, our visits
where no one takes us in their arms again,
where Polish children taunt us,
urinate on our families' graves.
and smoke like alcoholics.

YEARS LATER EUCHARIS MAGDALENE SPEAKS TO THE BLESSED VIRGIN

Perhaps I am being forward
but I must assume that you, too,
have felt a longing—
if not for Joseph, for something.
When the angel came, you were flattered,
but did you ever once imagine a different life?
My daughter shares your name if little else.
As a child she climbed willow trees,
hoisted her body ever closer to the warbler's nest.
She savored the marketplace,
elders haggling over well-fleshed carp.
Her hair was soft as a hoopoe wing,
brilliant as the Sea of Galilee.
Her lips, petals really,
spoke an earnest message no one cared to hear.
Men wanted to wake beside her.
Their women bore sons while Mary
bore the burden of unnecessary repentance.
After the Resurrection,
she remembered the sound of Him stirring in the morning,
sparrows in the eaves, a quiet sky
before gossip later at the open-air trough.
It was then she knew to leave the weight of Jerusalem behind her,
no sails to guide her across the Sea of Reeds.
As you will attest, miracles stand in plain view.
She pushed off beneath the light of Orion,
floated on benevolent pine,
fire coral and angel fish below.

AT THE GALLERY — HOUSE ON CRESCENT

Question: Can you tell us about the dark figures in the windows?

They are obviously the artist's parents. They were both dead
when the painting was completed. Although there are 7 windows total,
the deceased are on the first floor. 5 upstairs windows emit celestial light.

Question: Why does the sun consist of 3 spheres, each within the another?

Most of us never question the sun will continually rise and set
and rise again. Each sun within a sun represents a different stage of life,
just as the 3 black circles outlining each one represents its finite nature.
The artist wanted to believe in constants, but it is obvious she knew better.

Question: What about the spirals?

They symbolize the final birthday dinner—limp baked potato fries.
A disappointment to say the least. Memory typically served the artist well;
in this case imagination failed her. The good news is she never had to eat them again.

Question: Beyond painting, what inspired her?

Singing. As a way to remember. Notice the house leans away from the sun,
into the wind. Listen:
  I'm a rambler; I'm a gambler, I'm a long way from home.
  And if you don't like it just leave me alone.

YAK ON THE MOUNTAIN

Did you, too, see it plunging, head down, in a wild gallop across the steppes?
Did you see it against the ridgeline, before the forests of Silver Fir—
plump, white, tea plant beneath its sturdy limbs,
a steady balance of purpose and desire as it gazed upon
the monsoon valley? Did you think to brush the soft underhair
of its belly, spinning the short, fine fibers with silk,
until your sleeves were dressed like butterflies?
Did you see it then lumber beyond the shadow
of the Kullu valley, beyond the snow-capped peaks?
Did you hear it breathe into arid sky, a silent prayer,
riding the wings of the wandering magpie
to one who might listen?
And did you answer in a language you eventually understood?
Have you traveled far enough to look back?
And have you forgiven yourself?

FROM THE EDITOR

Yours is a poem waiting,
like the narcissus in my yard, to bloom.
Poor little buds are getting fooled.
I'm afraid they may blossom just in time for Thursday's frost.
And that, as you know, will end their short lives!
So your beautiful start is about being fooled.
But for a moment the narcissus will flower,
brilliant enough to give all who look upon it
a fleeting taste of spring. Yes!
Being fooled is the star attraction
— and your first stanza sings!

I just returned from a long walk where I thought about you
and your poem and how much I enjoy hiking
through winter and, as winter becomes spring,
how easy it is to be fooled.
How we are so easily given to promise.
I thought, too, about how we waste our very best years
trying to create meaning, how we hope
to balance the poet's desire with the publisher's standard
and end up mired in identifying orphan lines
abandoned at the bottom of a page
or kerning the space between characters
where meaning is often lost. In fact, we are
the narcissus in the yard,
pushing up through the frozen earth.
When finally we do break through,
how little time we have!
We should be grateful, I suppose,

for resolute buds that manage against all odds
to come between ambition and discovery.
What is our calling, after all,
if not to be astonished?

To see a World in a Grain of Sand
And a Heaven in a Wild Flower,
Hold infinity in the palm of your hand
And Eternity in an hour

—William Blake, *Auguries of Innocence*

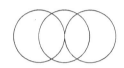

Still Life

Is it safe to put a pond in a poem?
How about a heron
at the shoreline, its leg lifted
like a mime over unsuspecting carp?
Is it safe to slip a snail in a pond
in a poem, spilling over with algae?
What about a promise? Will it float
like hope? Will it glimmer and flash
and arouse curiosity or worse?

I once slung a secret in a pond in a poem.
It grew a tail, a carapace, and bony plates,
a beak with a rough cutting edge.
It took on a life of its own,
ripped the legs right off a cricket frog
tore the head off a lotus,
spread rumors I never intended.

I wonder what a memory would do.
If I tossed it like a stone,
would it skip, sink, or swim?
Would it drown or dwarf or morph
into something more or less
like love,
like loss,
like regret?

What about sun on the surface, a kingfisher
diving for truth? The red-winged blackbird
so far away he's nearly
left the page?

Draw a timeline.   Begin
with your birth and your mother
who wove stories to bind you to her.
End with your death and ignore imagination.
You cannot forecast cause:
brain cancer or heart attack in the produce aisle.
Nor can you predict setbacks
like crying at your first job interview
and drinking too much afterwards.

A timeline allows you to visualize
significant achievements:
graduation, employment, your wedding day
and so on and so forth until many years later
when you learn about Andromeda
and other galaxies and their relationship to you.
Like your relationship to your mother
who will surely have died by then,
and on a particular date you will stop thinking of her
as your mother and instead think of her
like any other human being or something other
than human because eventually
she won't share any of the same qualities you have.
She will simply be energy at that point.
And you will ask yourself:
How does that kind of consciousness work?

But this poem is not about death.
This poem is about all the days before
or the lifetime that is a single, non-linear day,
whether measured in coffee spoons,
        or ocean tides and howling moons,
my own reticent longing to feel the pull of your neck
in my hands, this dream of a life we share,
physical and metaphysical in the bodies
we could not stop touching
as if we once believed this is all there is:
sex and skin, soft belly and the angle of legs
that now carry us on foreign bones.

The fact of the matter is
our bodies operate in total darkness.
All we have been permitted by nature,
or evolutionary biology,
or perhaps by God,
are two slight openings with which to see
everything.
Meanwhile one hundred trillion cells
and twenty thousand breaths
circulate inside you every day.

Even when you sleep,
even when you dream you are climbing
an ancient tree in your neighbor's yard
to reach for the magnolia blossom,
and your long monkey feet
wrap around the trunk, even as you fall
with a flower in your hand and your husband calls
from the kitchen and the smell of toast and coffee
is what you least expect in the cloud forest you fall from,
eighty-six billion nerve cells,
and one hundred trillion connections
—more than there are stars in the Milky Way —
scramble at two hundred miles per hour
over a distance of sixty-thousand miles,
twice the circumference of planet earth inside you,
to deliver this message in the dark:

wake up.

Sometimes you are afraid of what you do not know.
Sometimes you stand on the back patio at night,
look through trees and hear a colorless hum that hides
between whip-poor-will and memory,
soon lost in the babble of after-dark arias:
the grand nocturnal opera,
its principal players hiding all around you.
And you, in full view, the dunderhead.
This must be how the spirit feels,
long after its arrival
when the witless body betrays itself
and the two become strangers on a yearslong journey
to find each other again.

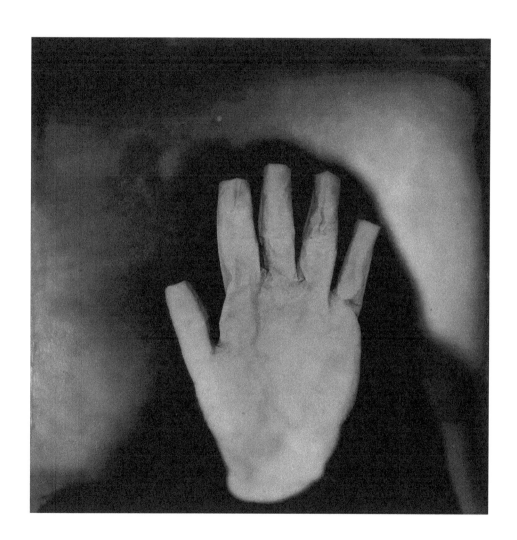

Fourteen thousand years ago
a star called Vela died.
You try to organize your days.
You can no longer organize your days.

A star called Vela died.
It rivered through the atmosphere and you
try to organize your days
by trees and lakes and ocean coral.

Whatever rivers through the atmosphere,
however random, is measured now
in trees and lakes and ocean coral.
What do you study for evidence?

Time is measured now by fitful
reminders of what you lost,
evidence of a life in hindsight:
round fingertips, nails bitten to the nub.

Reminded of what you have lost,
you imagine yourself without a body.
Round fingertips, nails bitten to the nub no more!
Your phantom breath is a temporary vestige.

Without your body, your limbs
are shattered stars blasting cosmic radiation
through every breath you ever took.
Time is a fourth dimension, a necessary coordinate.

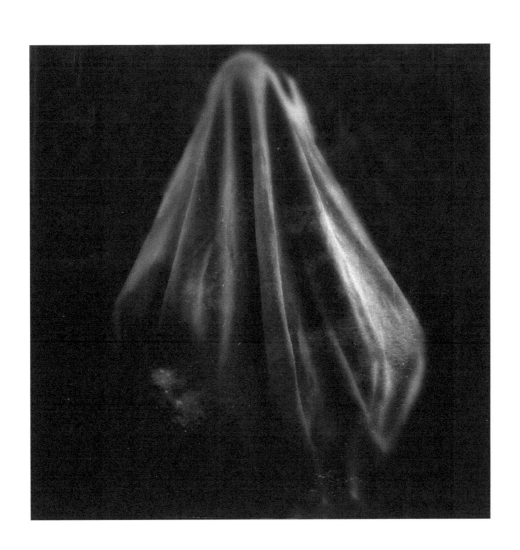

Shattered stars blast cosmic radiation,
turned by time, buried beneath sediment.
Time is a fourth dimension
that tells you where you are.

Buried by time, turned beneath sediment,
is proof of a star called Vela.
You miss the only coordinate that matters.
You can no longer organize your days.

If this day were a photograph,
no one would ask how you came to be here,
why she bellowed from beyond the frozen pond,
how you strained to see the unseeable
deep within the woods but stopped short
of entering alone.

You returned with the slick, black dog that ran ahead.
An injured doe had made her way across the dam.
She lay in shock beneath the falling snow.

One brown eye blinked to protect the smallest bit of her,
but the blood, which would not be veiled,
drained from her body and a gray mist drifted
toward the dog.

What point is fear — that distant pain
that bleeds its way toward lilacs
that will never bloom in her lifetime?

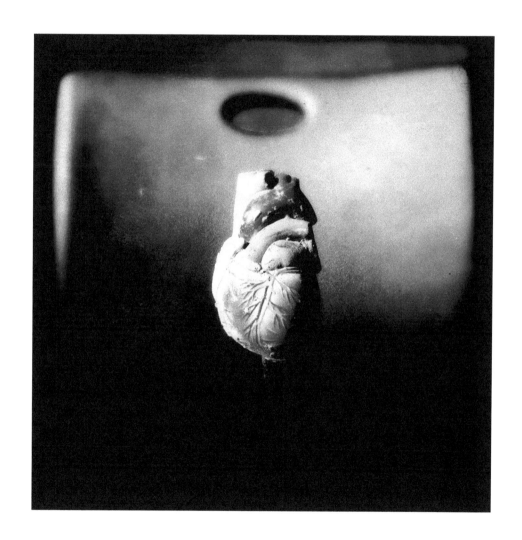

Instinct and imagination are different animals.
You have one and not the other.
You brought a dog to protect yourself
from what you do not know,
and you cannot smell the future.

In a few short months, male cardinals will call out
"birdie, birdie, birdie."
Goddamn ants will rise up from the soil,
and geese will line the shore.
It may snow in April,
but forsythia never panics.

You, on the other hand, walk down the lane
in winter and long for a different season.

Finches, doves, meadowlarks commence
their singing while cranes and killdeer

return unnoticed by longspurs and harriers
who, like you, are poised for a journey

you anticipate far too long.

Listen: can you hear it breathe
into arid sky, a silent prayer,
riding the wings of the wandering magpie
to one who might listen?

And can you answer in a language
you understand?

Have you traveled far enough to look back?

And have you forgiven yourself?

ACKNOWLEDGEMENTS

I thank the editors of the following publications in which some of the poems have previously appeared, sometimes in slightly different form.

Atticus Review: "Edouard Manet's *Olympia*, A Biography"

Asylum Magazine: "The Gift That Came Here"

I Thought I Heard A Cardinal Sing, anthology edited by Kari Gunter Seymour, Ohio Poet Laureate: "In The Direction Of Words"

The MacGuffin: "Chronesthesia: A Time Travel Poem," "What You Carry"

The Main Street Rag: "Consciousness As A Kind Of Relativity"

Northern Appalachian Review: "From The Editor," "Strange Bodies," "Meditation," "November," "Confession,"

Pikeville Review: "Yak On The Mountain"

Pine Mountain Sand & Gravel: "Corkscrew Willow," "Last Lesson"

Pudding Magazine: "Apology," "Absolution," "Parallax," "Is it Safe"

Shadelandhouse Modern Press, *The Bookrow Blog:* "Poem to My Younger Self"

Sheila-Na-Gig: "Forgiveness"

Typehouse: "Assignment," "Metaphor," "Refugees," "Aria"

Women Speak: 10th Anniversary Collection, anthology edited by Kari Gunter Seymour, Ohio Poet Laureate*:* "Druthers"

Women Speak, Volume Eight, anthology edited by Kari Gunter Seymour, Ohio Poet Laureate*:* "A Tale Of Two Women"

Special thanks to Virginia Underwood, publisher at Shadelandhouse Modern Press, for her guidance and support of this collection, to Jane Ann Fuller, my steadfast editor, who—through her keen eye and sensitivity to language—helped give birth to this book, to Pauletta Hansel who offered inspiration throughout the pandemic with her online workshops, to James Riley for his thoughtful and often humorous insights, to the Tuesday Poetry Group members who unfailingly provided feedback on my poems: Jane Ann Fuller, Wendy McVicker (Athens Poet Laureate), Bonnie Proudfoot, Jean Mikhail, Renee Williams, and Kristine Williams. Thanks to my husband, Mark Hackworth, for helping push my metaphors to their limits and for the many engaging and occasionally heated discussions about art and aesthetics. Finally, thanks to my younger sister, Deb Anderson, who has always been the oldest, has provided ongoing encouragement, and has attended every one of my readings!

Additional thanks to Jane Ann Fuller, my epistolary partner in poetry, for lines borrowed in the poems "What You Carry" and "Chronesthesia" and to Jacqueline Boyle for the beautiful quote from her Time Travel Journals that appears in the epigraph in "Chronesthesia".

ABOUT THE AUTHOR

DENI NAFFZIGER is the author of five books including *Strange Bodies, Desire to Stay, Still Life*; *Revenants: A Story of Many Lives* (co-authored, funded by The Ohio Arts Council), and a children's coloring tale, *A Story of Flying,* which was produced for the Passion Works exhibition, *"A Story of Flying,"* and was funded by The Ohio Arts Council. She has also published three chapbooks: *Desire to Stay* (The Spoon River Quarterly), *Close to Home* (Crazy River), and *Intervals* (Pikeville Review). Her work has been published in many literary magazines and journals, including *New Ohio Review, Atticus Review, The MacGuffin, Pine Mountain Sand & Gravel, The Main Street Rag,* and others. For nearly twenty years, Naffziger edited *Riverwind*, a national literary publication (Hocking College, Nelsonville, Ohio.) She earned a Fulbright Scholarship in 1990 and taught Creative Writing and Advance Literature at Kendal College in Kendal, England. She has over thirty years of experience teaching creative writing and disability studies. Naffziger currently serves as Poet-In-Residence at Passion Works Community Studio in Athens, Ohio.

Printed in the USA
CPSIA information can be obtained
at www.ICGtesting.com
LVHW071344091023
760302LV00002B/4